FORT JEFFERSON
AND THE
Dry Tortugas National Park

L. WAYNE LANDRUM

Wayne Landrum

ACKNOWLEDGMENTS

For over six years I lived at the Dry Tortugas, experiencing first hand the rich natural and cultural history of the park. During this time, I came in contact with many people who shared their knowledge and love for the area, both past and present. Their insights, along with my research and experiences, have given me a special appreciation for this magnificent place. Space does not permit me to list all my contacts and their contributions, but I wish to thank the following persons for their generous support and help.

For assistance in locating historic photographs: Nancy Russell, Curator, Everglades National Park; Tom Hambright and John Brown, Monroe County Library, Key West, Florida; and natural history association employee at the Dry Tortugas, Eloise Pratt.

For review of the draft manuscript: Everglades Chief of Interpretation & Visitor Services, Cherry Payne; Dry Tortugas ranger Mike Ryan; wildlife biologist, Sonny Bass, from Everglades National Park, John Viele, the author of a series of books on the Florida Keys; Monica Woll, a local naturalist from Key Largo; and my son, Casey Landrum.

I also wish to thank Larry Murphy, Chief, Submerged Cultural Resource Center, National Park Service for the use of NPS underwater photographs. Special thanks go out to photographer Janet Eldridge-Taylor for use of her beautiful photographs, and Craig Howard for his creative talent in the layout and design of the book. Lastly, I thank my wife, Kathy, for assisting me by editing the book and for the use of her photographs.

Front Cover: Aerial view of Garden Key - Kathy Landrum
Back Cover: Daybreak at the fort - Kathy Landrum

Published by / Copyright ©2003 L. Wayne Landrum
178 Sandy Circle, Big Pine Key, FL 33043

Design and Typography: Fonts & Film, Key West, FL

Printed in China

ISBN: 0-9742158-0-5

Library of Congress Control Number: 2003094735

et Taylor

Janet Taylor

CHAPTER 1
THE DRY TORTUGAS

There is a special place, at the end of nowhere, but on the way to everywhere, a place of explorers, pirates, smugglers, soldiers, prisoners and scientists. This is a place where some men lost all hope, and many died in despair. Though pain and suffering contributed to its fascinating history, it is also a place of beauty, vivid colors, peace, solitude and happiness. Abundant wildlife live in the clear turquoise sea, rainbow-colored coral reefs, and on the white sandy islands and beaches. This is a place where sea birds rule, sea turtles thrive, and coral reefs and sea grasses provide for a rich diversity of ocean plant and animal life. This is Dry Tortugas National Park.

DISCOVERY

Located in the Gulf of Mexico, 70 miles west of Key West, the Dry Tortugas are the westernmost part of the Florida Keys Reef Tract, 90 miles north of Cuba, 200 miles south of Tampa Bay, and just 70 miles north of the Tropic of Cancer. The park consists of seven small sandy coral islands, which together cover only about 97 acres of dry land. These islands are surrounded by shallow rocky coral reefs, sandy ocean bottoms and sea grasses. They comprise a paradise rich in natural and human history. Although small in size and remote from civilization, this place has been an important part of history since discovery, in 1513, by Don Juan Ponce de León.

Upon his arrival, Ponce de León and his Spanish crew found the area teeming with wildlife. There were large numbers of birds and sea turtles, which provided fresh eggs and meat for food. Seals were also present and easily taken for food. Since there was no refrigeration, sea turtles were important to mariners of the day. These large creatures could be rolled on their backs and kept alive aboard ships as a continuous source of fresh meat. Ponce de León captured about 160 turtles, 14 seals, and more than 5,000 birds for food on his journey. He named the islands "Las Islas de Tortugas," (The Islands of Turtles) for the hundreds of turtles found there. Later, "Dry" was added to charts to alert mariners that there was no fresh water on the islands.

Today, the birds, fish, and sea turtles are still abundant on and around the islands, but the seals are gone. The seals living in the Dry Tortugas were Caribbean monk seals that once ranged throughout the Caribbean Sea. They were hunted and easily caught for food, until they became a rare species. An island resident reported seeing a few of the seals living in the Dry Tortugas as late as 1908, and the last confirmed sighting anywhere was in 1952. This species was declared extinct in 1996.

GEOLOGY

The Florida Peninsula underwent dramatic changes during the last 100,000 years. Rising and falling sea levels caused major changes in the size and shape of the area. During the Wisconsonian period, 18,000 years ago, glacial ice reached its maximum extent on the North American and European continents. The climate was extremely cold and the polar ice caps grew in size.

nrise brings another day to this remarkable place.

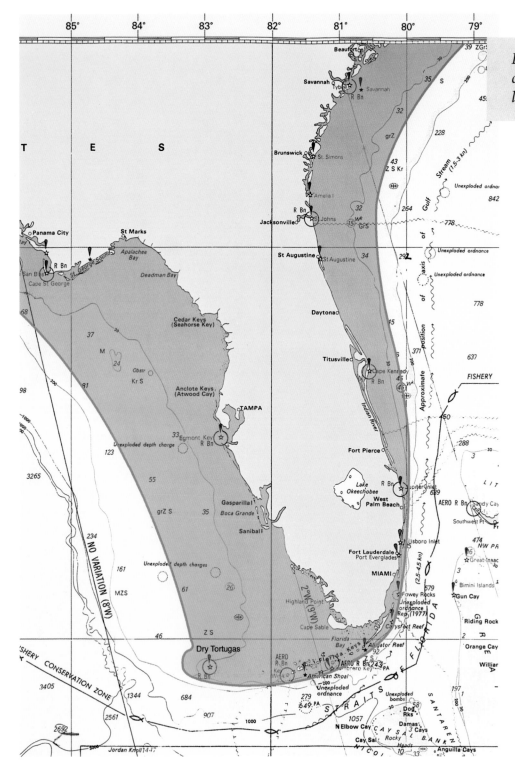

During the last 15,000 years the sea level has risen about 350 feet. This elevation change has made the Florida peninsula half the size it once was. The previous land mass is indicated on this chart in green.

With water locked in ice, the sea level dropped 300 to 400 feet below its present level, exposing the broad flat Floridian Plateau. The place we call Florida was twice the land size it is today, as more of the continental shelf was exposed. The Florida Keys were not islands then, but were part of the continent. During that time, it would have been possible to walk on dry land to the Dry Tortugas.

About 15,000 years ago, a warming period began. Ice began to melt and gradually the seas began to rise. Over a period of 5,000 years the sea rose about 350 feet. This rate of rise slowed over time, and during the last 2,000 years, the sea level has risen only about 6 feet.

Coral reefs began to form as the sea reclaimed the land. Bank reefs and patch reefs grew in the shallow seas along the coast of south Florida, on top of ancient reef deposits, to become the Florida Keys Reef as we know it today. The reef tract is about 200 miles long with its northern end near Miami, curving south and west, terminating at the Dry Tortugas. The keys west of Key West, including the Dry Tortugas, are known as the "sand keys." They consist of carbonate sands, lying on top of the deeper Pleistocene reef formations.

THE ISLANDS

Scientists began to study the area in the early 1830s and fortunately, have provided us with documentation of changes at the Dry Tortugas for the past two centuries. One of the scientists, Alexander Agassiz, surveyed the shallow reef formations, sea grass beds, and the eleven islands existing at the time. His map, published in 1882, provided a valuable reference for the documentation of changing conditions in the Dry Tortugas.

By 1900, three of the islands, Sandy Key, North Key and Southwest Key,

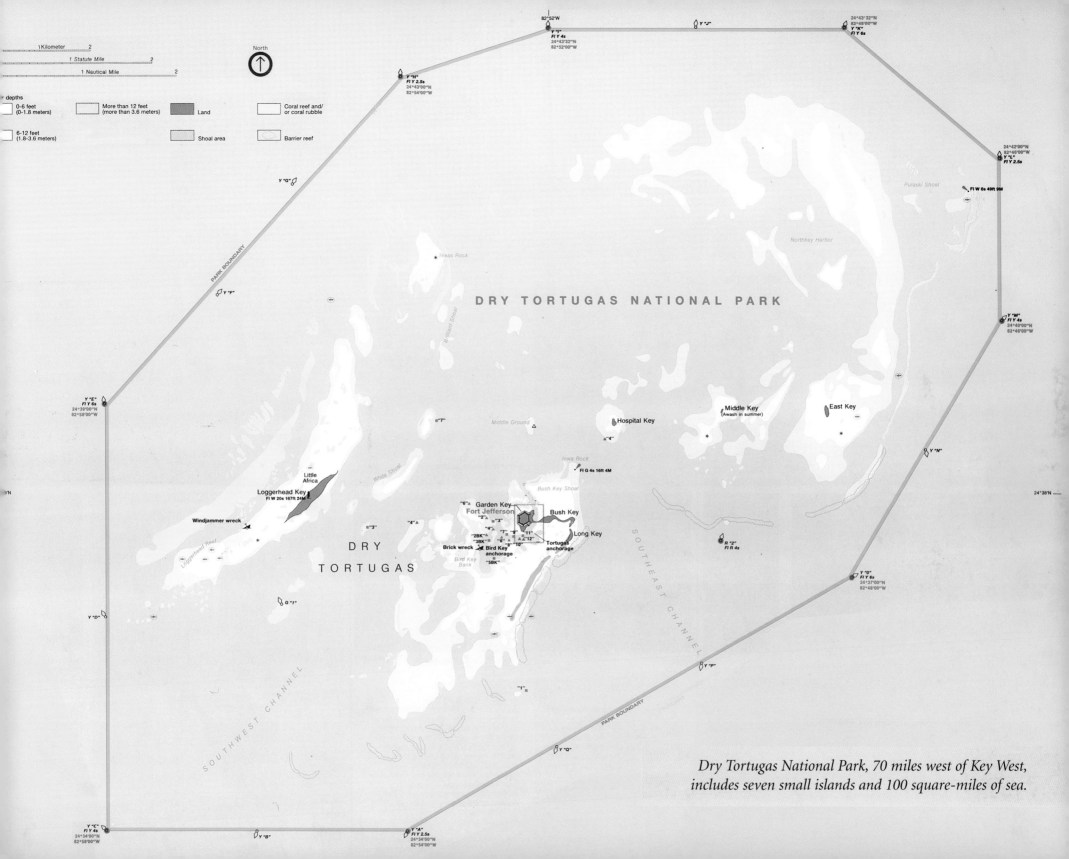

Dry Tortugas National Park, 70 miles west of Key West, includes seven small islands and 100 square-miles of sea.

Janet Taylor

Janet Taylor

were reclaimed by the sea. Bird Key, just southwest of Garden Key, once a major nesting site for sooty terns, washed away in the 1930s, probably due to hurricane activity. One hundred years after Agassiz published his map, scientists returned to survey and map the area again. By comparing the two maps, it was observed that many changes had occurred. Four islands had washed away, but the surface area of the remaining seven islands stayed about the same as the original eleven. The sand from the disappearing islands may have shifted to the remaining islands. Other changes had occurred in the coral reefs. The staghorn and octocoral hard bottom area increased in size and the living staghorn corals had declined significantly.

Of the remaining islands, Loggerhead Key is the largest. Covering about 49 acres, it is the site of Loggerhead lighthouse, constructed in 1857. It was also the location of the "Tortugas Laboratory," built and operated by the Carnegie Research Institute, for tropical research, from 1904 until 1939.

Garden Key covers about 22 acres and is the site of the first lighthouse built in the Dry Tortugas in 1825. Fort Jefferson dominates the island with its towering walls and huge parade ground. It was used intermittently by the military from the 1840s until the early 1900s. Today, it is the operations center for the park and the focus of most human activity in the Dry Tortugas.

Bush Key, just east of Garden Key, is about 20 acres in size, and was once called Hog Island because hogs and cows were kept there as food for residents of the fort. After Bird Key washed away in the 1930s, the colony of sooty terns began nesting on Bush Key and today, it is the home of the only nesting colony of sooty terns in the continental United States.

Long Key, about an acre in size, is south and east of Bush Key. It has a dense cover of mangrove trees and supports the only remaining nesting

Kathy Landrum

colony of magnificent frigate birds in the continental United States.

Hospital Key, a very tiny island north of Garden Key, was used in the mid-1800s for a temporary hospital during yellow fever epidemics. It is also unique in being the only known nesting site for masked boobies in the continental United States.

East Key, as denoted by its name, is the easternmost island of the Dry Tortugas, and covers about 4 acres. It was not developed in any way, and is the best example of native vegetation and natural conditions existing when discovered.

Middle Key, a small tidal island between Hospital Key and East Key, is the smallest of the islands. It often washes away in the summer and reappears during the stormy winter months. It has no vegetation, but is a popular gathering place for sea birds.

Changes continue to occur in the size and shape of these sandy islands. In the 1980s, the gap between Long Key and Bush Key closed and the two islands connected. In December of 2000, Bush Key connected to Garden Key, as the sands shifted and filled the channel between the two islands.

Wayne Landrum

9

CHAPTER 2
EARLY HISTORY

From the time of discovery until the present, the islands of the Dry Tortugas have been an important landmark for passing ships. These small islands, located at the northwest entrance to the Florida Straits, were the first lands sighted when arriving from the west. Spain and Portugal began running great galleons loaded with gold, silver, and precious gems from Central and South America. The treasure fleets discovered the fastest way back to Europe was by sailing through the Gulf of Mexico to Cuba, stocking up on provisions at Havana, then continuing east through the Florida Straits. By doing this, they could take advantage of the Gulf Stream, a very strong current in the ocean flowing from the Gulf of Mexico into the Atlantic Ocean.

EARLY DISASTERS

In 1622, one of the worst early disasters of a Spanish treasure fleet occurred near the Dry Tortugas. After leaving Havana for Spain, a deadly hurricane struck the fleet; three of the treasure galleons and six other ships wrecked in the storm. The *Nuestra Senora de Atocha* and *Santa Margarita* sank, and the *Nuestra Senora de Rosario* was blown aground in the Dry Tortugas. A search expedition from Havana found the *Rosario*, and rescued the crew and passengers and salvaged the treasure. The other ships sank, taking 500 sailors and passengers to a watery grave on the bottom of the sea, along with the cargo of gold, silver and emeralds.

Subsequent Spanish expeditions salvaged some of the treasure from the *Santa Margarita* during the next three years, but the *Atocha* remained lost in the shallow seas until its discovery by Mel Fisher in 1985. A salvage company has recovered much of the lost treasure and continues to search for more. Both of these wrecks are outside the boundary of Dry Tortugas National Park.

The first documented use of the Dry Tortugas for fortification occurred in 1742, and was quite by accident. While England and Spain were at war between 1739 and 1748, their warships roamed the area of the Florida Straits. A 50-gun British ship, the HMS *Tyger*, was patrolling the area west of Cuba with orders to capture or destroy Spanish ships. The captain of the *Tyger*, Edward Herbert, took his ship with a crew of 280 men north into the Gulf of Mexico searching for Spanish ships.

On January 12, 1742, the *Tyger* ran aground on shallow reefs in the Dry Tortugas, and the crew was unable to haul their ship off the reef. Fearful of being discovered, the captain ordered the crew ashore in small boats to a nearby island (Garden Key). During the next several days they carried supplies and water from the ship to the island and began building fortifications on the island. Crewmen removed cannons from the ship and placed them on shore behind makeshift defensive barriers.

A passing Spanish ship finally discovered the stranded *Tyger*. The Spanish crew removed a mast from the *Tyger* to use as a replacement, and sailed away, only to return two days later. Some of the British crewmen were on board the *Tyger* removing supplies for their island fortification. When they saw the Spanish ship approaching, they set the *Tyger* on fire to prevent it from being looted. It burned to the waterline. A later attempt was made to

ggerhead Key is the largest island in the park and its beaches are an
portant nesting area for the loggerhead sea turtles.

Once discovered, the Dry Tortugas became a landmark for sailing ships passing through the Florida Straits. This ship is the replica of the HMS Bounty, and occasionally sails through the park.

board and capture the Spanish ship with a surprise attack from their small boats, but they were driven back.

Weeks passed, and the marooned crew of the *Tyger* was getting low on water and rations. Finally, one of the *Tyger's* small boats that had been sent to scout the area to the east found an abandoned sloop, repaired it, and sailed it back to Garden Key. This was great news to the captain and crew who had now been on the island for 60 days. They now had enough room in their small boats and the larger sloop to escape the island. They disabled their cannons, threw them into the sea, and sailed away. Their 700-mile journey to Jamaica was successful, though it included many narrow escapes as they sailed south and west around Cuba. This ended the first known fortification of the Dry Tortugas, but it was certainly not to be the last. This saga is described in detail by John Viele in, *True Stores of the Perilous Straits.*

PIRATES

"His stories were what frightened people worst of all. Dreadful stories they were: about hanging, and walking the plank, and storms at sea, and the Dry Tortugas, and wild deeds and places on the Spanish Main," wrote Robert Louis Stevenson describing his pirate character, Long John Silver, in the fictional book, *Treasure Island.*

One can certainly imagine the brash swashbucklers, daggers at their sides, lying in wait in these islands, drinking rum and preying on the rich treasure and cargo ships passing through the Florida Straits.

The Spanish, French, British and Dutch fought to control the lands and seas of the Caribbean and the Gulf of Mexico. For over 300 years, pirates and privateers (private vessels that hired out to opposing countries) attacked and robbed treasure and merchant ships heading to and from their homeports. The pirates often used fast shallow-draft vessels to strike the larger slower ships, which they could out-maneuver and then escape into the shallow waters of the Dry Tortugas and other keys. There is little early record of the use of the Dry Tortugas as a base for ships, but the Dutch West India Company's privateer fleet, commanded by Admiral Piet Heyn, cruised in the vicinity of the Dry Tortugas while lying in wait for Spanish *flotas.* Protected waters from the natural harbor in the Tortugas provided shelter for ships from storms, and allowed them to repair and maintain their vessels. Throughout the years, privateers and pirates probably took advantage of the fine harbor, as indicated by the remains of ships run aground or sunk in the shallow reefs and waters.

Spain claimed all of Florida from the early 1500s, and Florida and the Dry Tortugas were also under the British flag at one time. In 1763, during a war with Spain, the British captured Havana and demanded Florida in exchange for Havana. Spain relented and gave up all claims to Florida for the return of Havana. In the Treaty of Paris (1783) at the end of the Revolutionary War, the British returned Florida to Spain to prevent the United States from claiming it.

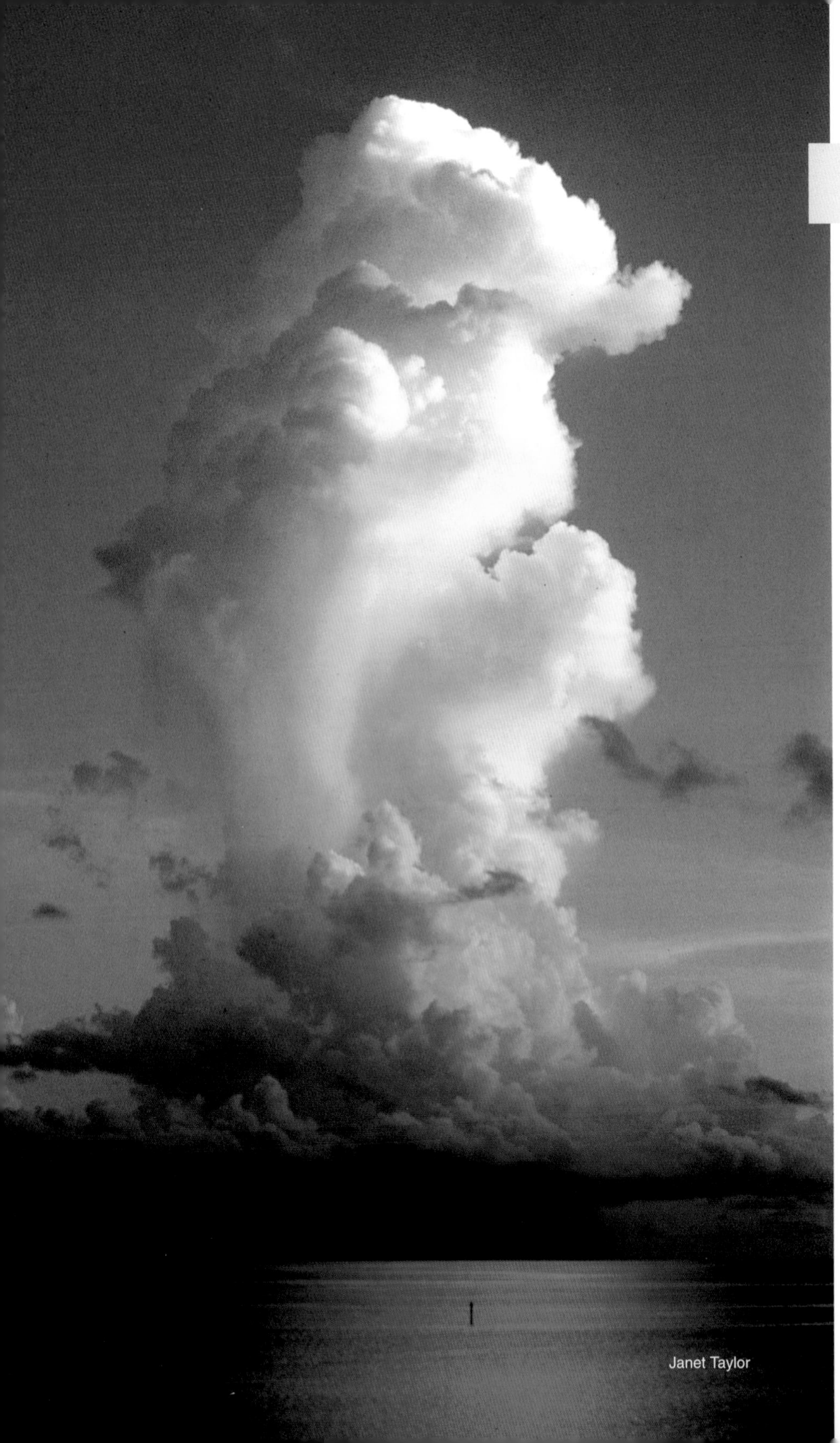

In 1821, Spain ceded Florida to the United States for five million dollars, and settlers began to move into the new territory. The Spanish, in 1815, had granted Juan Pablo Salas, a Spanish artillery officer, ownership of Key West. John Simonton, from New Jersey, bought the island from him in 1822 for $2,000. Simonton sold three fourths of the island to others, and development began.

After the War of 1812, piracy increased rapidly in the area as thousands of military men and seamen lost their jobs and turned to freebooting (plundering). The United States Congress established a navy squadron in Key West to chase them down. Captain David Porter, a naval hero of the War of 1812, led the squadron. He began using fast shallow-draft vessels to pursue and attack the pirates, and the threat of piracy was gradually reduced in the region.

WRECKERS

The Dry Tortugas and other islands in the Florida Keys are surrounded by shallow water with coral and rocks. This, combined with strong currents, frequent storms, poor charts, and crude navigational instruments, made this area a graveyard of wrecked and grounded vessels.

There are over 250 documented shipwrecks or "casualties" in the Dry Tortugas, dating from the 16th century to the present. These marine disasters represent an international collection of ships that flew flags from countries throughout the world.

Janet Taylor

13

The Windjammer is one of over 250 documented shipwrecks in the park. (left)
A grounded shrimp boat greets the rising moon. (right)

With all the shipwrecks and groundings happening along the Florida Keys, the industry of salvage operations began. The first known salvors were the natives, living in the Keys, who treasured the gold and silver as ornaments, then later learned of their value. The Spanish often employed natives to assist in the recovery of valuables from grounded and sunken ships because of their excellent swimming and diving abilities. The people depending on shipwrecks for their livelihood, by assisting grounded vessels and salvaging their cargo, became known as "wreckers."

Wrecking became the main industry in Key West, and the federal court there was the only court in the United States authorized to license wrecking captains and their vessels, and to revoke those licenses for misconduct. When a ship or vessel was aground or in danger of sinking, the first wrecker on the scene would seek permission to assist, and the captain of the ship in need of help could either decline or accept the assistance. If accepted, the first wrecker on the scene became the "wreck master" and supervised the operation. The salvage fee was determined by the court, dependent upon factors such as degree of risk or injury to the wreckers and their vessels, the weather and sea conditions, location of the wreck, the value of the cargo, and skill required for the job.

Wreckers were required to assist during emergencies and many of them, while waiting for wrecks to occur, fished for additional income and subsistence. Wreckers would often anchor in the Dry Tortugas waiting for vessels in distress.

LIGHTHOUSES

After the area became a territory of the United States, the U.S. Lighthouse Service began to build lighthouses in the Florida Keys to help

National Park Service

prevent ships from running aground. In 1822, Congress authorized a lighthouse to be built on Garden Key. Construction of the 70-foot tall lighthouse began in 1825, along with a resident keeper's house. By 1840, with shipwrecks continuing to occur, it became apparent that the lighthouse was not effective. It was not bright enough or tall enough, and it was too far away from the other shoals and reefs.

In 1856, a taller lighthouse was authorized and construction started on Loggerhead Key. Towering 152 feet above the island, it was made of brick, with walls 8 feet thick at the base. A lighthouse keeper's house was built, along with a separate smaller house used for a kitchen and assistant lighthouse keeper's quarters. The lighthouse is still in use today, but has been automated and powered by solar panels. The keeper's house burned down, but the smaller, two-story building, is still used today to house park employees.

The original lighthouse on Garden Key continued to operate until it was seriously damaged by hurricanes in 1873 and 1875. By the time the lighthouse was removed Fort Jefferson had been under construction for 30 years.

By 1876, the Lighthouse Board approved the construction of a new lighthouse on top of the southeast bastion of Fort Jefferson to replace the Garden Key lighthouse. Iron was used to build the tower since brick could shatter and spread flying debris into the fort if hit by cannon fire. The use of iron also made it possible to build a sturdy, yet comparatively lightweight structure that required minimal surface area- important factors considering the tower's location. The new lighthouse, with a height of about 75 feet, was designated as a "harbor light."

Wayne Landrum

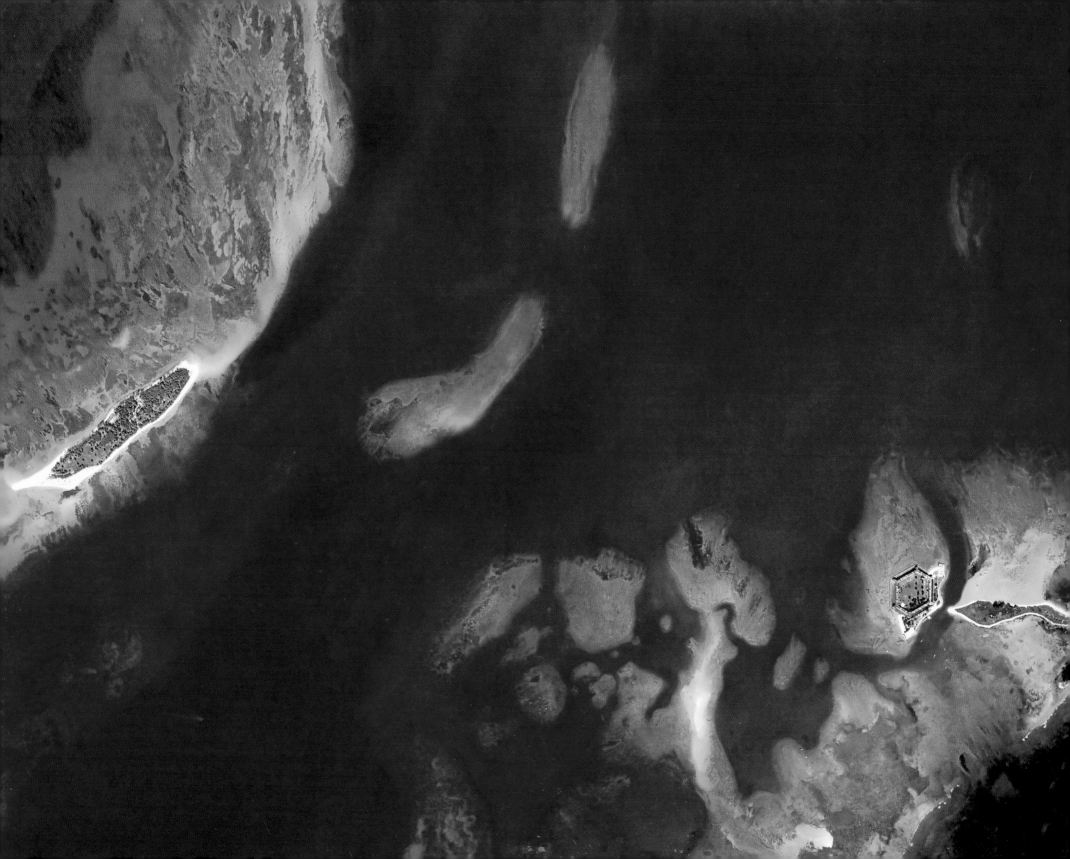

CHAPTER 3
COASTAL DEFENSE PROTECTION

Soon after becoming a new nation, President George Washington established a series of coastal defense forts along the East Coast. These early forts, historically referred to as part of the "First System" of forts, were started in the late 1790s to protect the country from Great Britain, France and other countries. After the threat of war passed, they were abandoned and eventually fell into decay. A "Second System" of forts, with improved defensive walls and better armaments, was planned and implemented in the early 1800s.

In the War of 1812, between the United States and Great Britain, the British pillaged and burned Washington D.C. The United States was made painfully aware of a need to improve its defense from seaward attack, so a more advanced design of forts was developed, called the "Third System." These new fortifications were made of stone, brick, concrete and other materials. Bigger and better cannons had been developed and were installed inside and on top of their thick walls. The early war ships could not successfully attack these forts now armed with superior firepower.

RECONNAISSANCE

This new series of coastal fortifications was planned along the coast of the United States from the Atlantic to the Gulf Coast States, and eventually, the coast of California. A fort at a location in the Dry Tortugas was considered as a possible addition to the system. Navy Commodore David Porter was instructed to do a reconnaissance of the islands. He toured the area in 1825 and was not impressed. Porter reported the islands were low,

sandy, and liable to changes from gales of wind. He wrote, "they have a good inner harbour for small craft and a tolerable outer one for ships of war; but they have no fresh water, and furnish scarcely land enough to place a fortification on and it is doubtful if they have solidity enough to bear one."

Four years later, the veteran naval officer Commodore John Rodgers made a stop at the Dry Tortugas to check the area out again as a possible defensive site. Unlike Porter, he was delighted at what he found and reported that the inner harbor, "would be safe in all seasons and was large enough to allow all the navies of Europe to ride at anchor."

He added that the geographic location was perfect, and, if fortified, the Dry Tortugas could be the "advance post" for the defense of the Gulf Coast. Commodore Rodgers also noted that the islands were directly in the track of all vessels going between the Mississippi River, west Florida, and all the eastern coastal states.

After reviewing the John Rodgers report, the U.S. Navy ordered a detailed survey of the Dry Tortugas. Lieutenant Josiah Tattnall, leader of the survey, supported the findings of Rodgers, and further stated that the harbors were deep enough for the largest ships and were free of rocks, with good holding ground. Tattnall also pointed out that the British, French, Spanish, and Danes had colonies in the Caribbean. These island possessions were "said to be well fortified," while the United States had no naval base along the Gulf Coast.

he area between Garden Key and Loggerhead Key is a deep basin suitable for
choring ships, so it was chosen as the location for a coastal defense fort.

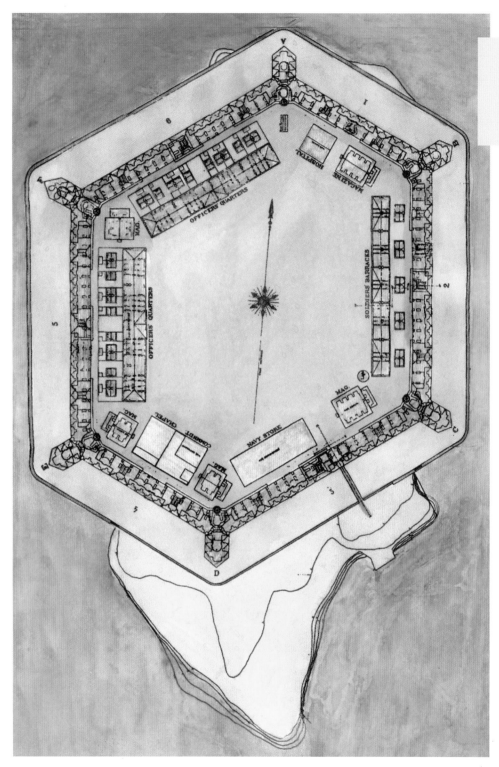

A Fort is Planned

A young, growing United States was expanding its land base in the Gulf, with the Louisiana Purchase, in 1803. Settlers along the Mississippi began to ship goods down the river to New Orleans and around the tip of Florida to the East Coast. With this flood of trade goods, it became important for the United States to establish a defensive position at the Dry Tortugas to protect vessels shipping from the Gulf Coast states through the Florida Straits to the Atlantic states, and on to Europe. It was of equal importance to fortify the Tortugas to prevent another power from taking it.

The plan for the fort was to provide a safe storage depot for enough materials capable of sustaining the land and naval forces charged with the defense of the Florida Reef for one year. The fortification was also to provide a safe harbor for warships, and facilities for repair of the naval squadron.

Guns of the time had a limited range, and any ship could simply sail out of the range of the fort, but its real value was to provide protection for warships in the huge natural anchorage. Commodore Rodgers and Lieutenant Tattnall mentioned in their report the strategic location of Dry Tortugas for a fort and as a coaling station. By providing water, supplies and munitions to ships at this location, days could be saved from having the ships return to the mainland. The fort was also designed to have enough large guns to protect any attack on vessels seeking shelter in the harbors.

The first congressional appropriation for construction in 1844, was signed by President John Tyler. Garden Key was selected as the island to be fortified because it was closer to the anchorage than the larger Loggerhead Key. Garden Key, with its various channels, was also more easily approached by sailing vessels in any wind direction. In 1845, by Executive Order, President James K. Polk proclaimed Garden Key a military reservation.

Wayne Landrum

The fort has over 2000 brick arches.

Under the leadership of Chief Engineer Joseph Totten and the U.S. Army Corp of Engineers, the fort was designed as an elongated hexagon, with four sides measuring 477 feet long and two sides at 325 feet, to be made of brick and masonry, and surrounded by a moat 70 feet wide, with a seawall. The fort was to be composed of three tiers rising about 45 feet above water level. It was designed for 420 heavy guns and howitzers. The protective sea wall, with a perimeter of half a mile, was to surround the fort with only one entrance. A large amount of granite was needed for its construction, along with timber to build forms and scaffolding. The fort design incorporated over 2,000 brick arches, and was designed for a garrison of 1,500 men.

Lieutenant Horatio G. Wright of Connecticut, a graduate of the U.S. Military Academy, was appointed to supervise construction. He purchased a 112-ton schooner, *Activa,* and arrived on Garden Key in December, 1846. He described the area as, "eight islets, covered with mangroves, bay cedar, cactus, and buttonwoods with dazzling white sand beaches." Garden Key was barely three feet above sea level, 300 yards long by 200 yards wide, with a stagnant pond in the center. Upon his arrival, the only full time residents were the lighthouse keeper and his family.

George Phillips, a "master mason" from Buffalo, New York, accompanied Wright. Phillips spent the next 20 years overseeing the fort's construction, and much of the credit for the superb arches and workmanship goes to him. He left Fort Jefferson, to become the caretaker of Fort Zachary Taylor in Key West, another coastal defense fort constructed at the same time.

FORT CONSTRUCTION BEGINS

Upon Lieutenant Wright's arrival, the first order of business was to establish quarters for the work force and to obtain required materials for this

National Park Service

enormous project. The only construction material on site was plenty of sand and coral rubble, which could be used to mix with cement. All other construction materials had to be shipped in from many far away places on slow moving ships and barges. This included large amounts of bricks, cement, lime, iron, lumber, granite, and slate.

Cement for mortar, slate for roofing and gun-room floors, granite for stairs and gun ports were shipped down the eastern seaboard from New York and Vermont. Most of the lumber for scaffolding, forms, and other woodwork came from Jacksonville, Florida, before the Civil War. Tons of iron were shipped in from various places for drainage pipes, construction beams, and ordnance related munitions such as Totten shutters, embrasures and traverse rails.

Waiting on supplies often took months, and necessary appropriations for funding even longer. Hundreds of ships and barges made the hazardous trip from many distant seaports, carrying thousands of tons of material needed for this huge fortification. Storms sometimes caused the ships to sink or run aground, forcing additional set backs to the construction. Many of the supply ships were lost to the dangerous Florida reefs, often wrecking and sinking, some within sight of the fort. All other supplies, including most of the food, clothing, and other equipment had to be shipped to this remote location.

In the first stages of construction, a type of northern red clay brick was used, but it failed to hold up well in the hot, humid subtropical environment. In July 1854, a change was made to use southern bricks from brick companies near Pensacola, Florida. This larger orange brick was harder and superior in its ability to stand up to the harsh climate of the Dry Tortugas. Later, during the Civil War, when brick was unavailable from southern states,

the Union project again turned to northern brick to cap the top layer of the fort. This smaller red brick is easily seen throughout the upper sections of the fort. Overall, an estimated 16 million bricks were used during construction.

Fresh water was critical to the fort's operation, residents and passing ships. Fort Jefferson was built with over 100 cisterns to catch and store the average yearly rainfall of about 30 inches. Rain falling on the fort roof was filtered down through sand to drainpipes and into the cisterns, beneath the fort floors. The cistern capacity under the fort was 1,500,000 gallons. An additional cistern was built in the parade ground under a proposed chapel foundation, with a capacity of 92,000 gallons. The chapel was never finished, but the cistern is still in use today. Water distilling plants were added later to make fresh water from the sea, to supplement the rainwater.

On October 8, 1850, after almost four years of construction, Secretary of War Charles M. Conrad selected the name, Fort Jefferson, in honor of Thomas Jefferson, the nation's third president and principal architect of the Declaration of Independence.

Under Wright's direction most of the foundation work was completed and the first tier was started. In 1857, a new superintendent engineer, Captain Daniel Woodbury, replaced Wright. Woodbury was recognized as a leading authority on wall and arch construction. At that time, there were 299 workers including: 148 laborers, 58 slaves, 68 masons, 7 carpenters, 2 smiths, 2 stone cutters, a physician, overseer, 8 crewmen, and 4 utility men. There were also a few women and children on the island.

WAR THREATENS

Captain Montgomery C. Meigs replaced Woodbury in 1860. This was an important time in the fort construction because of the impending Civil War. Meigs had traveled to this new assignment through the southern states. He observed the dangerous mood of the citizens he encountered, and the extreme hostility throughout the south in this presidential election year. At every stop on his way, he was told that the southern senators intended to resign "if Mr. Lincoln is elected."

Upon his arrival at Key West, his anxiety increased on hearing Florida Governor Madison Perry's demand for possession of the United States' public works within the state. Captain Meigs became even more apprehensive when he arrived at Fort Jefferson and found not a single cannon at the fort.

Meigs ordered the closing of all the openings in the fort walls and made the drawbridge over the moat, at the entrance to the fort, operational.

Rumors were that Fort Jefferson and Fort Taylor were to be taken by the South. Meigs requested Commander John M. Brannan at Fort Taylor to send guns and ammunition to Fort Jefferson. Captain Meigs was elated on the 18th of January when the steamer, *Joseph Whitney,* arrived in the harbor with 66 officers and men of Company C, 2nd U.S. Artillery, under the command of Major Lewis G. Arnold. They were under orders to occupy and protect Fort Jefferson.

Major Arnold went back to Key West and returned with enough guns to partially arm the fort, along with another gunboat, the *Crusader.* When they arrived at the fort, the Union gunboat, *Mohawk,* rode at anchor in the harbor. Times were changing rapidly as the fort geared up for a possible war. On January 10, 1861, Florida seceded from the Union and the secessionist forces had already seized the unoccupied coastal fortifications at New Orleans, Mobile, Pensacola, Savannah and Charleston. Ironically, one of the reasons for building the fort was to protect the southern states along the Gulf of Mexico, and now, it was to support a blockade to strangle the rebellious South.

CIVIL WAR BEGINS

In 1861, the Civil War began with the first shots fired by Confederate troops on Fort Sumter, near Charleston, South Carolina. The brutal saga of war between the North and the South began to rage. Fort Jefferson, with its strategic location as a defensive outpost and supply depot for the United States, now changed direction in history. It was caught up in the bitter Civil War. The fort, occupied by the Union forces, provided anchorage, supplies, and protection for the warships blockading the South. By the end of 1861, 65 guns were mounted in the fort, from 24-pound howitzers to 8-inch

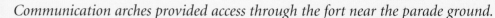

Wayne Landrum

columbiads. There were also on hand, but not mounted, 41 additional guns. In the first year of the Civil War, there were about 400 people living in the fort, including workers, soldiers, prisoners, and some family members.

During the Civil War, the two most southern forts, Fort Jefferson, at the Dry Tortugas and Fort Taylor, in Key West, remained in Union hands. Fort Pickens, near Pensacola, Florida, also remained in Union hands throughout the war. The rest of the state withdrew from the United States. Key West, accessible only by boat, was now in a unique situation. With the presence of Federal troops, most of its 3,000 residents willingly or unwillingly stayed in the Union. Key West became the headquarters of the East Gulf Blockading Squadron where blockade runners, when caught, were brought into federal court.

In March 1862, a full regiment of nearly 1,000 soldiers from New Hampshire and New York arrived on the island. This brought the number of people living on the island to over 1,400. Fresh water was a recurring problem and condensers were ordered to make fresh water from the sea.

MILITARY PRISON

Fort Jefferson became a military prison shortly after the beginning of the Civil War. The Union needed a place to put prisoners, and the fort was isolated and well protected, so ships began to bring in convicted soldiers. The first 33 prisoners arrived in September 1861. By November 1864, the prison population peaked at 882 prisoners, and at the end of the war, in 1865, there were 768 prisoners. Almost all the prisoners were Union soldiers who were sent to the Dry Tortugas as other prisons began to overflow. The prisoners were serving time for all types of charges ranging from desertion and murder, to petty crimes and misdemeanors such as theft, or disobeying

Janet Taylor

orders. Sentences varied from a few months, to 99 years, or life in prison.

Most of the prisoners were assigned to the Engineer Corps to assist in fort construction, which was still in progress. Except for some of the more serious violators and troublemakers, most were treated about the same as other workers. They were generally allowed to go about the fort, except at night when they were confined to their rooms. Many escape attempts were made. Some were successful, but most escapees were caught, and some died in their attempts.

Fort Jefferson was a busy place during the Civil War. The anchorage was used as a refuge and staging area by warships and many other vessels. Garden Key had a military store for purchasing limited provisions and supplies. All supplies were shipped in, except for locally obtained seafood and bird eggs.

The Civil War came to an end with the surrender of Robert E. Lee and his army on April 9, 1865. News of Lee's surrender arrived at Fort Jefferson by the steamer, *Corinthian*, on April 12. Two hundred guns were fired to celebrate the end of the war, but the celebration didn't last long for the people living at the fort. A few days later the vessel, *Ella Morse*, came into the harbor with flags at half-mast, bringing the tragic news that President Lincoln had been assassinated on the night of April 14. Following the end of the war, prisoners were still sent to the fort, as it remained a prison for several years.

CIVILIAN PRISONERS

While almost all the prisoners were military, one group of four civilian prisoners drew a lot of attention: the Lincoln assassination co-conspirators. After the assassination of President Lincoln by John Wilkes Booth at Ford's Theater, Booth fractured his leg jumping to the stage from the presidential

Wayne Landrum

Dr. Samuel Mudd, a prisoner, assisted in the care and treatment of patients during a severe outbreak of yellow fever. He was later pardoned from his life sentence.

to serve a life sentence in prison. Little did he know he would eventually be sent to the prison at Fort Jefferson.

Three other people charged in the conspiracy were also sentenced to prison at Fort Jefferson along with Dr. Mudd: Edward Spangler, Michael O'Laughlin and Samuel B. Arnold. Dr. Mudd and the other three civilian prisoners arrived at Fort Jefferson in the summer of 1865. Two months later, Mudd attempted to escape from the prison.

Prisoners often assisted in loading and unloading supply ships, and it was during one of these work details that Dr. Mudd hid aboard a ship, hoping to escape from the island. However, to his dismay, he was missed and a search began. He was soon found and brought back into the fort. For several weeks after his escape attempt, he was shackled and closely guarded.

In a letter to his family, he described his escape attempt: "My dear Jere: I wrote to you and Frank by the last steamer, but at the same time intended to arrive before it. Providence was against me. I was too well known and was apprehended five or ten minutes after being aboard the steamer. They were so much rejoiced at finding me, they did not care to look much farther; the consequence was, the boat went off and carried away four other prisoners, who no doubt will make good their escape."

AN ENGLISH PRISONER

Another well known prisoner was an Englishman, George St. Leger Grenfel, who was from a wealthy family, and ran away from home at the age of 17 to become a soldier of fortune. He fought wars around the world in Africa, India, Turkey, and South America. Grenfel was in his late fifties when the Civil War began and he headed to the United States after remarking, "If England is not at war I go elsewhere to find one." He met with General

box. He escaped on horseback and stopped early the next morning at the farmhouse of Dr. Samuel A. Mudd, seeking medical treatment. Later, Booth left the house of Dr. Mudd and after several days on the run, was finally trapped in a barn by a cavalry detachment. He was shot and killed after a standoff.

Dr. Mudd was arrested within a few days after treating Booth and charged along with several others for conspiracy in the death of President Lincoln. There was, and still is to this day, much controversy into the role played by Dr. Mudd in the death of the president. Dr. Mudd stated that he did not recognize Booth when he stopped by his house for treatment of his broken leg. He and several other alleged civilian conspirators were put on trial in a military court. Four of those convicted were sentenced to death and hanged, but Dr. Mudd missed the death penalty by one vote. He was ordered

Soldiers often camped and trained in the parade ground. (right)
Late 19th century supply ship at north coaling dock. (below)

National Park Service

Robert E. Lee to offer his services. He then joined Morgan's raiders in Kentucky, where he trained Confederate troops in cavalry tactics and horsemanship. He also fought alongside these southern troops, often leading them into battle.

After leaving Morgan's raiders, Grenfel went to Washington and convinced Secretary of War Edwin M. Stanton that he had retired from the Confederate army and would provide information about the Confederacy in exchange for free travel in the north. He proceeded to make secret plans with the Northwest Confederate Conspiracy to capture Chicago and release southern prisoners at one of the prison camps, which was holding 15,000 men. Betrayed by an informant, Grenfel was caught and sentenced to be hanged as a spy. President Andrew Johnson, Lincoln's successor, commuted Grenfel's sentence to life imprisonment at Fort Jefferson. He arrived at the fort in June 1866. He was described by Emily Holder, wife of the fort surgeon as, "a ferocious looking man six feet tall, black hair unkempt, long beard, with black eyes under very heavy eyebrows....He wore a red flannel shirt open low on his chest showing a strong muscular figure, trousers tucked in his high boots, altogether having the appearance of a bandit....He violated all rules and regulations, so was naturally often in the guardhouse....He carried his broom over his shoulder with as lordly an air as though he was a Viking with his battle axe."

His defiant attitude coupled with an abusive lieutenant named Robinson, caused him to be punished often. At one point he was tied outside the fort to bake in the horrendous hot sun, then, with rocks tied to his feet, he was thrown three times into the water to the mercy of the sharks. He survived each time. Finally, after surviving all this, he was left on the dock overnight to recover.

National Park Service

National Park Service

Early 20th century fort visitors stand along the "cannon ball trail" to the officers quarters from the sally port. (left)   After many decades of crowded living conditions, solitude returns to the fort. (right)

A new commander, Major Valentine Stone, came to the fort and sent Lieutenant Robinson to Key West to stand trial for abuse of prisoners and soldiers alike. Grenfel befriended the new commander and his position improved. Unfortunately for him, the new commander died of yellow fever.

YELLOW FEVER STRIKES

A severe outbreak of yellow fever struck the fort residents in 1867. At that time, there were 400 people living in the fort, including 54 prisoners. By September, 270 of the residents had been stricken . Dr. Joseph Smith, the fort surgeon, was one of the first to die. His young son followed days later. All four hospital nurses died of the dreaded disease. Following Dr. Smith's death, Dr. Mudd volunteered to take over the medical duties. Grenfel worked with Dr. Mudd in the care and treatment of those stricken. By the end of the

yellow fever outbreak in November, 38 people had died, including Mrs. Valentine Stone, the wife of the fort's commander. Major Stone left the fort with his infant son, but both died in Key West. Both doctors at the fort at the time, Dr. Mudd and Dr. Edward Thomas, were sick by October, but survived.

After the epidemic passed, a recommendation was made to obtain a pardon for Grenfel for his efforts. Though he fully expected one, his application for clemency was denied in January 1868. Now in his sixties, he realized he might never get released, so on the night of March 7, 1868, he and three other prisoners made a daring escape in a small stolen boat. That very same night, a violent storm hit the Dry Tortugas with high winds and heavy rains. Grenfel and the other prisoners were never heard from again.

By the end of the Civil War, the number of people living at the fort began to decline. Prisoners and soldiers were being released and sent home. In 1869, President Johnson pardoned Dr. Mudd and Samuel B. Arnold. Dr. Mudd had been sentenced to life at hard labor, but when pardoned, had spent just less than four years incarcerated at Fort Jefferson. He returned to his farm in Maryland, and died in 1883 at the age of 49. Edward Spangler, when released, returned to Maryland and lived out his life on Dr. Mudd's farm. The fourth accused conspirator, Michael O'Laughlin, died at the fort during the 1867 yellow fever epidemic.

Landrum

CHAPTER 4
LIFE AT THE FORT

Life at the fort during and just after the Civil War has been well described by some of the people who lived there. A person's outlook was directly dependent upon why they were there and the season of the year. There were two main seasons. For six to eight months, in the winter and spring, the weather is pleasant and cool; in the summer months, it is hot, humid and muggy. Summer was the time of illness and the possibility of outbreaks of the dreaded yellow fever. No one knew the cause of yellow fever. Only in the 1880s did scientists discover that the disease was caused by a virus and transmitted by a species of mosquito.

EMILY HOLDER

One of the best accounts of life at the fort during the Civil War came from Emily Holder, the wife of the assistant surgeon and one of the few women at the fort at the time. She kept a detailed journal, which was published by *The Californian* in 1892. Upon first arriving at the fort with her husband in 1858, she wrote, "our first view in the early morning as we sailed in through the winding channel was surely suggestive of a prison. Over the top of the fort we caught sight of trees and the roof of a building with a tall, white lighthouse towering over all. The little keys that we had passed some pure white, others with a few trees and shrubs, took away something of the isolated feeling. Three miles away stretched out the largest of all these islands except the one on which the fort was built on which was another larger lighthouse. The exterior of the fort was bare and repulsive, the interior offering a decided contrast. Here were trees of the deep green belonging to tropical vegetation, so restful to the eye in the glaring sun; and as the walls enclosed about thirteen acres, and water could not be seen, I instinctively lost the feeling of being so far from the mainland."

She went on to describe the fort, "on the inside showed long stretches on each curtain of arches making pleasant places for walking, cool and shady; and in the moonlight the effect was really beautiful. Looking not unlike some grand old ruin with its lights and shadows, one could invest it with all sorts of romance."

During the arrival of Union troops to protect the fort from possible attack in January 1861, Emily wrote, "Already our quiet life was a thing of the past. The large guns came from Key West, were soon mounted and began to feel as though we were on a war footing."

By March 1861, life at the fort changed as Emily noted, "We numbered at that time about four hundred, and represented a busy little town. The fort at night was brilliant with lights, and the place was active with the bustle of many people." In June of the same year she wrote, "the census was taken, showing that 550 souls were living on this sandbank of thirteen acres, too large a number we deemed for safety, little thinking that before long Fort Jefferson would be the home of several thousand men." A year later, Emily again described the increasing numbers of soldiers, "There never had been more that five or six companies on the island at one time, and there were no accommodations for more, yet here came a full regiment of one thousand men and the question, Where should they be quartered? was a serious one. The parade was quickly converted into an impromptu camp-ground; tents

...am ships and sailing ships continued to bring supplies, soldiers and ...soners to the fort.

were pitched, guns stacked and, as if by magic, camp-fires appeared with men sitting around eating, their knapsacks serving as tables, or reading the letters they found awaiting them."

There were very few women and children at the fort during the war. Emily Holder describes a 4th of July party in 1862, "After dinner we adjourned to the piazza and heard the Colonel deliver a patriotic speech to the soldiers, who were drawn up in line before headquarters. Then we went home for an hour or so, returning for a hop, at which there were present twenty gentlemen and eight ladies. The latter were scattered about so as to look as numerous as possible, and as we had all put on evening dress, some one said they might be deluded into the belief that it was another party."

When prisoners began to arrive in large numbers, she showed her dismay by writing, "On the twenty-third we saw a steamer over the ramparts and concluded that the exchange (of command) had come, but to our great disgust it proved to be one hundred and seventy more prisoners, really there seemed a prospect of the fort being turned into a penitentiary."

Emily Holder described depressing times when break-bone fever, possibly a mild form of yellow fever, broke out and almost everyone living at the fort was sick. "The heat was intense, the silence oppressive beyond description: there were no soldiers for drill or parade and the gloom was indescribable. We were all ill at the same time with no physician: five hundred at one time would scarcely cover the list of those ill with the fever; thirty out of one company and all its officers, while those who were able to move about looked like ghosts."

OTHER VIEWS OF LIFE AT THE FORT

Warren L. Stebbins, an army private with the 110th N.Y. Volunteers, provides a glance at a soldiers life in a letter home, dated April 16, 1864, "A strict enforcement of military law is necessary here for our own safety for there are a large number of prisoners here for various crimes with penalties in regard to time varying from three months to ninety nine years or for life. Quite a number have a ball and chain to their legs for company. I must confess I have but little relish for such an ornament."

Soldiers spent their time off fishing, catching turtles, and collecting seashells and bird eggs. Stebbins describes the birds, "On some of the Islands the guls [sic] lay large numbers of eggs at this season of the year. Three men from each Co are permitted to go fishing every day—they sometimes secure large numbers of these eggs and we cook them. They are in some respects different from hens eggs but are a very good substitute for soldiers." (These were probably the sooty terns that continue to return each year to nest.)

Many people died during the Civil War years at the Dry Tortugas. Burials were reported on several of the keys, including Bird Key and Hospital Key. Stebbins writes, "Last night there was a soldier of the 110th died. His name was Evarts of Co. H. He is the 7th of the Regt. that have died since the Regt. came here. None of the soldiers hat [sic] die here on this Island are buried here but are taken to an island east of here about six miles called East Keye."

Lincoln conspirator and prisoner Samuel Arnold had a very negative view of the place. He wrote, "Without exception, it was the most horrible place the eye of man ever rested upon, where day after day the miserable existence was being dragged out, intermixed with sickness, bodily suffering, want and pinching hunger, without the additional acts of torture and inhumanity that soon I became a witness of."

The soldiers also had some good times as described by Samuel Horner, in a letter home about a July 4th celebration, "What did you do on the 4th of July? We had big times here. The first thing in the morning wes [sic] the firing of 36 cannons at sunrise. Then a game of baseball at 10 o'clock, at 12 noon climbing a greased pole, prize $10, after which the firing of 36 guns, 200 pounders. At 2 pm, a sack race, prize $7. The way they done it they got into sacks and tied them stick out and theim [sic] run for 200 yards. The next was a wheelbarrow race, for $10. That was done by blindfolding the racers and letting them run at a dog trot toward a pole. The one that went the straightest won the prize. Next was the pig race. They greased a pig all over with soft grease and let him loose. The first one to catch him got the pig and $7. (He was about 3 months old.) The next was a crib race for $10. The men got in wash tubs and paddled with their hands. The first one out won. At night they had fireworks and a stage dance."

During the Civil War there were hundreds of soldiers and prisoners living in crowded conditions, suffering from the hot climate, boredom, and a poor diet. In January of 1865, there was a great deal of sickness among the prisoners from the effects of scurvy, caused by a lack of vitamin C. Dr. Joseph B. Holder, the fort assistant surgeon, sent for limes from Key West and fed

Nathan Lan

The interior of the fort, with its large shaded parade ground, provided a relief from the hot exposed exterior of the fort. (left) Historical re-enactors in period clothing. (right)

Janet Taylor

the men vegetables and a local plant, purslane, to improve their health. The prisoners received rations only after the Engineer Corps, the officers, and the soldiers.

In order to earn money to keep the prisoners supplied with the limes, the doctor came up with the idea of a theater troupe of minstrels made up of prisoners and soldiers. The doctor's wife, Emily, described the beginnings of the theater, "he issued an order that every body that could sing a song, tell a story, dance a jig, perform tricks of any kind should report at his office the next morning. The motley forlorn, disconsolate-looking crowd that gathered the following day would have inspired an artist. They had no idea of anything pleasant for them, and were so wretched and hopeless they looked more as if they were going to an execution, than recruits as a nucleus of a theatrical performance."

Emily continued, "The Doctor said it was most amusing to watch the expression of their faces as he began to divulge his scheme; and when they really understood that he was going to do something for their benefit, it was magical. Some who had crawled up the stairs as though they were literally on their last legs, before the conference was over had danced a hornpipe or a jig; others had shown their skill at gymnastics; songs were sung, and the talents displayed was almost an embarrassment of riches, while the crowd could scarcely be recognized as the moping, listless one that came in."

With little else to do, they were eager to participate in the theater. Twenty-five cents was charged for admission to the performances from fort personnel and ships' crews, who were passing through. Known as "The Key Lime Theater," it was such a success and so popular it provided not only funds for medicine, food, and limes, but an outlet for comic release and entertainment for those involved as well as the audience.

Kathy Landrum

CHAPTER 5
AFTER THE CIVIL WAR

After the Civil War, construction continued at the fort with attention given to the completion of the officers quarters and barracks. Then, in 1873, there was yet another outbreak of the dreaded and deadly yellow fever. Before the epidemic ended in September of that year, 37 more people contracted the disease and 14 deaths were reported.

This was only the beginning of a bad year. In October, a hurricane, the third in seven years, struck the fort. The barracks were badly damaged, the hospital lost its roof and the slaughterhouse and stable were swept away, along with 19 cattle. Almost all the military personnel left the fort, leaving behind the Engineers Corps to repair the damage. Then, another hurricane blasted the Florida Keys in 1875, causing more damage to the structures at the Dry Tortugas.

WRIGHT RETURNS

In 1876, Horatio G. Wright, who had worked on the fort as superintendent in 1846, returned to the fort. He was now a Colonel with the Board of Engineers for Fortifications, and came to conduct an inspection with Colonel Zealous B. Tower. They reported that the fort was essentially finished except for the second tier embrasures. Some of the large rectangular spaces, intended for gun ports, had been filled in with a thin brick wall dating back to the Civil War when the casemates were used as barracks.

They also reported that the fort's big guns were in excellent condition, but the iron embrasures were badly rusted. Other areas needing completion were the officers' quarters, barracks, detached magazines and chapel. Some

work continued over the next few years, but by 1884, with one ordnance sergeant on duty, the place was rusting and crumbling away. Congress was not interested in paying for repair of now-obsolete fortifications and weaponry. Masonry forts could no longer withstand bombardment from new, more powerful rifled cannons.

QUARANTINE STATION

Additional damage to the fortification came with yet another hurricane in 1886, and a severe storm in 1888. The army lost interest in the fort, and transferred it to the Marine-Hospital Service as a quarantine station in 1889. The station was to inspect and disinfect vessels bound for the United States from Cuba, the West Indies, and Central and South America. Vessels were boarded and inspected for diseases and those that did not pass the inspection were quarantined and disinfected. An annual report in 1897 stated, "during a 12 month period 63 vessels were boarded, 12 were inspected and passed, and 51 disinfected and held for observation."

In 1899, a description of the disinfecting process was provided by the troop transport, *Florida*, bringing soldiers back from Cuba to the United States. The transport pulled into the quarantine dock at the fort and the troops promptly disembarked, and the soldiers' blanket rolls and knapsacks were inspected, "All fabrics were bundled in the blankets, the bundles stenciled, and then placed in the steam chamber. The ponchos were placed in piles by companies, and dipped in a solution of bichloride of mercury by station employees...tents, cots, etc., remained in the holds and were

nnons lined the top of the fort in the late 1800s.

Wayne Landrum

positioned to permit fumigation by sulphur dioxide. Uniforms of officers were placed in staterooms and disinfected by formaldehyde gas." The process with this one ship alone took three days and one would have to wonder, with all the chemicals used, what dangers the treatment posed?

THE SPANISH-AMERICAN WAR

By the late 1890s, Spain was losing its hold on Cuba. Tensions mounted between Spain and the United States. In January 1898, the battleship U.S.S. *Maine* weighed anchor near the Dry Tortugas and steamed across the Florida Straits to Havana. While at anchor in the Cuban harbor, it blew up and sank on February 18, killing 260 of the 355 men on board. With this emotional event, the United States recognized Cuba's independence from Spain and declared war on Spain.

During the Spanish-American War, the quarantine station was suspended, but the lab and hospital remained open for disinfecting warships, troop transports and soldiers. In the third week of February, nine of the wounded survivors from the battleship *Maine* were brought to the fort and hospitalized. Warships and torpedo boats were still coming into the anchorage for water and supplies. Six Navy seamen were treated during the summer for yellow fever. One young seaman died and was buried on Loggerhead Key. By 1898, only four companies of the Fifth U.S. Artillery were assigned to the fort. The Spanish-American War was over by the end of the year and the quarantine station was busy disinfecting troops returning by ship from Cuba. Cuba became an independent nation in 1902.

The buildings inside the fort began to fall apart from neglect. (right)
In 1898, the Navy began building two large warehouses to provide coal
for warships. (below)

THE NAVY TAKES OVER

The Navy began construction of a coaling station on Garden Key in 1898 to support the war effort in the Gulf of Mexico and the Caribbean. The state-of-the-art station included piers, docks, conveyor belts and large coal sheds. The quarantine hospital remained on Garden Key when the Marine-Hospital Service begrudgingly turned over possession of the station officially on November 15, 1900. On December 23, 1900, the Naval Reservation of Dry Tortugas became part of the Naval Station, Key West, Florida.

By 1901, a detachment of marines was stationed at the fort. The harbor was dredged around the coaling docks, 30 feet deep and 300 feet wide, to allow the large ships to come in for coal. Large coal sheds, piers, and loading conveyor belts were in place and operational on July 1901. Records indicate that between 1904 and 1905, nearly 20 tons of coal was delivered to the new warehouses on Garden Key.

FORT JEFFERSON IS ABANDONED

All went well for the coaling station until October 1910, when the Dry Tortugas was struck by a severe hurricane. Following the hurricane, an inspection revealed major damage to the officers' quarters, barracks, coaling stations and docks. The decision was made by the Navy not to spend any more money on repairs and to abandon the coaling station. Arrangements were made over the next few years to remove any property of value and salvage scrap metal and bricks from the fort.

This left Garden Key, once again, almost empty except for a few people, including the lighthouse keeper. In 1912, a fire started in the keeper's outhouse. Fanned by high winds, the fire spread through the parade ground, burning down the keeper's house and gutting the barracks.

Dry Tortugas, Fla. North Pier + Shed. July 1, 1902.

Janet Taylor

Once abandoned, the fort and coaling docks began to erode and rust away in the salty, windy environment. Passing boaters and fisherman used the harbors, roamed the deserted fort, fished, collected bird eggs and hunted for sea turtles, just as in earlier days. Solitude and the lonely cry of sea birds echoed through the empty corridors, replacing the sounds of man's previous occupation.

LATER MILITARY USES

Fort Jefferson was used again by the military during World War I as a seaplane base and wireless radio station. During World War II, the harbor was used by torpedo boats, minesweepers and convoy escort vessels to protect against German submarines. During the first and second world wars, many of the coastal defensive forts were modernized. This involved severe changes to historical structures. Fortunately, Fort Jefferson did not suffer any of these new upgrades and appears much as it did when abandoned, with the exception of the interior quarters. In the 1960s, the National Park Service razed the officers quarters and the barracks because of their poor condition and potential safety hazard.

ry Landrum

Janet T

CHAPTER 6
DISASTERS

The Dry Tortugas, with many low lying islands, shallow seas and rocky reefs, have posed a hazard to mariners since discovery. Hundreds of ships have run aground or sunk in this 100-square-mile area in the last 500 years. Many ships were rescued or salvaged, but those abandoned have been ravaged by storms, salt water and ocean currents and reduced to rubble, rotted away, or covered over by coral reefs.

SHIPWRECKS

The most interesting and intact shipwreck in the park for visitors to see is the windjammer wreck, also known as the *Avanti*. It was an iron-hulled sailing vessel, 261 feet long, with three tall masts and displaced 1,862 tons. This type of sailing vessel was in direct competition with steam powered ships of the era, the late 1800s. The *Avanti* was en route from Pensacola, Florida, to Uruguay, with a cargo of lumber when it ran aground and sank on the reefs, in 1907, just southwest of Loggerhead Key.

This spectacular, well-preserved wreck has attracted a large population of colorful reef fish and larger fish, such as tarpon, barracuda, and large grouper. Beautiful soft and hard corals grow on and around the wreck. It lies in 21 feet of water, with its bow rising just above the surface. Information on the wreck and its location can be obtained at the visitor center in Fort Jefferson.

Another very interesting shipwreck is the Bird Key brick wreck, which lies in about 6 to 8 feet of water, and is located about a mile from the fort, in the Bird Key Harbor. This shallow draft vessel, 100 feet long was propelled by a large four-bladed propeller. Underwater archaeologists estimate its date of construction back to the 1850s. Much of this wreck was salvaged, leaving little evidence of its design, but its unusual propeller remains intact.

Before snorkeling and diving within the Dry Tortugas, check with park personnel on safety issues and important regulations. When diving, snorkeling or swimming, watch for approaching storms and powerful currents. Even on a calm day, currents can be very strong due to changing tides.

HURRICANES

The waters of the Straits of Florida between Cuba and the Gulf of Mexico have a long history of hurricane activity and tropical storms. The Dry Tortugas are located in this area, often called "hurricane alley." Over the years, changes have occurred on these low islands, barely 4 feet above sea level, as tropical storms and hurricanes batter the area. The islands constantly change shape with shifting sand and vegetation destruction.

From 1875 to 2000, about 135 hurricanes have battered Florida. Many of these passed over or near the Dry Tortugas, and some have caused extensive damage to the fort and other structures. They have also caused the loss of life to people living on the islands and in boats in the surrounding waters. In 1919, a hurricane passed directly over the Dry Tortugas killing an estimated 500 people aboard ships in the Gulf of Mexico.

Recent hurricanes to hit the Dry Tortugas were Donna in 1960, Alma in 1966, Georges in 1998, and Irene in 1999. Irene just brushed by, with little effect on the park. Hurricane Georges made a direct hit on the park with winds exceeding 100 miles an hour along with heavy pounding rain. In any

orms and hurricanes are common visitors to the small unprotected islands, osing them to high winds and pounding waves.

This steel sailing ship ran aground and sank in 21 feet of water in 1907. (left)
Winds and waves from hurricane Georges batter the fort and moat wall. (right)

National Park Service

given year the park has an estimated 15 percent chance of being struck by a hurricane.

The author was living at the fort with his wife and 20-month-old son during Hurricane Georges. There were about 15 park employees and family members, a work crew, and two park volunteers there at the time. Everyone decided to stay at the fort and ride out the storm. Preparations were begun by implementing the park's hurricane plan, (a written guide of procedures for hurricanes). The office equipment was covered, windows and doors were boarded up in the office building, visitor center, work buildings and employee housing. All loose outdoor equipment including picnic tables, outdoor furniture, recreational equipment and boats were secured.

Sandbags were filled and placed in the open gunports of the electric power plant to prevent seawater from damaging the generators. The safest place in a hurricane at the fort are the dark dungeon-like, powder magazines on the second floor of the fort, known as "hurricane caches." Two of these rooms, surrounded by 8-foot brick walls and filled with supplies and emergency equipment, are designated shelters. After tracking the storm and its intensity, everyone decided to ride the storm out inside their own individual brick quarters within the fort walls.

Hurricane Georges struck on the morning of September 25, 1998, with pounding waves on the moat wall and wind roaring through the fort's openings and corridors. It was a direct hit and before the wind gauge blew down during the storm, it recorded wind gusts up to 107 miles per hour. Heavy rains poured from the sky. Everyone stayed inside their residences until the afternoon. When the eye of the storm passed directly overhead, the wind died and the rain stopped. Then everyone went outside to see the result of the first half of the hurricane. Patches of blue sky were overhead, the wind

Landrum

Wayne Lar

The fort is completely surrounded by a moat wall, which helps protect it from pounding waves during storms. It also provided a water barrier and wall to prevent attackers from charging the fort by boat or on foot. (left)

An archaeologist mapping the remains of a sunken ship. (right)

was silent and there were hundreds of water puddles everywhere. The Dry Tortugas was a very wet place! Thousands of birds that had been dragged along by the storm began flying into the parade ground and landing on the ground, in trees, and along the fort walls, seeking shelter from the winds they had been fighting and a place to rest.

About two hours later after the eye passed, the winds began to blow from the opposite direction and everyone went back inside, as the second half of the storm began. During the night, the winds sounded like a continuous freight train roaring through the fort walls, blowing the rain sideways in torrents. By dawn, the winds began to cease and the rain slowed. The storm was over for the residents of the Dry Tortugas, but it continued on to strike the mainland. Everyone safely survived the hurricane at the fort. The fort, with its tall thick walls and shallow surrounding seas, is probably as safe as any place to be in the Florida Keys during a hurricane.

Following the hurricane, inspection of the place revealed some damage to roofs, docks, and water damage to quarters. There were many trees uprooted in the parade ground and on Loggerhead Key. The heavy rains from the hurricane formed a fresh water pond in the parade ground. Several hundred waterfowl, mostly blue-winged teals, swam around in their temporary home. Other birds, including many species of warblers, were everywhere, so exhausted they could be picked up off the ground, from within the fort casemates, and out of the bushes. Many of them died over the next few days, but most of them, after resting a few days, were able to fly away to their distant destinations. Had the hurricane not passed over the islands of the Dry Tortugas, the birds would probably have remained trapped in the eye of the hurricane over the ocean, and many more probably would have perished.

CHAPTER 7
TURTLES, BIRDS AND REEFS

Many changes have occurred since Ponce de León first visited the Dry Tortugas, almost 500 years ago. Humans have left their mark on these beautiful islands with the construction of Fort Jefferson, the lighthouses, and the ships that brought people to the islands to live, to look, and to work. Visitors and residents have had a variety of experiences there and many stories to tell about this place, leaving it rich in history. Scientists came to study the diverse natural history, including birds, sea turtles, ocean fish, and living coral reefs in this group of small sandy islands. Today, with modern transportation and an increasingly crowded world, even more people are attracted to this remote paradise.

SEA TURTLES

"Las Tortugas" was the Spanish name given to these islands for the sea turtles commonly found swimming around the islands and nesting on the sandy beaches. These giants of the sea, once sought for their meat, eggs, and beautiful shells, are now protected in this country and are excitedly searched for by people hoping to catch a glimpse of these magnificent creatures swimming nearby.

Sea turtles have roamed the seas for 150 million years. These ancient reptiles lived when the dinosaurs roamed the earth and were able to survive after the dinosaurs disappeared. They spend their life swimming in the sea, with the females crawling ashore only to lay eggs. The low sandy islands of the Dry Tortugas provide excellent nesting places of undisturbed beach area where they can continue their life cycle. There are only about 5 miles of sandy beaches that provide a place for turtle nests in the Dry Tortugas, but they are some of the most successful nesting areas in the Florida Keys.

Female turtles usually come ashore to nest at night, often on the full moon, in the months of April through September. They are an impressive sight as they crawl up on the beach, leaving deep tracks with their flippers as they plow through the sand. Using their large bodies and strong flippers to move sand, they dig deep pits above the high tide line, deposit the ping-pong-ball-sized eggs, and cover them, before lumbering back into the sea.

The incubation period for sea turtle eggs averages 56 days, and the last nests of eggs usually hatch by late October. The temperature of the sand helps determine the sex of the baby turtles. At temperatures of about 85 degrees, the eggs in a nest will be close to 50% male and 50% female. Higher sand temperatures increase the number of females in the nest while lower temperatures produce more males. Consequently, in the warm temperatures of the Florida Keys, most hatchlings are females; along the cooler Carolina coasts, most hatchlings are males. Watching these large reptiles nest, or the newly hatched baby sea turtles scamper to the sea, is an experience remembered for a lifetime.

The two common nesting sea turtles in the Dry Tortugas are the green and loggerhead species. Green turtles may weigh up to 450 pounds; loggerheads may weigh 350 pounds. Close monitoring of the Dry Tortugas nesting sites over a period of several years revealed that the loggerhead turtles average about 200 nests a year with about 100 eggs per nest, while the green turtles average about 40 nests a year with about 120 eggs per nest. Not

reat blue heron rests on the fort walls.

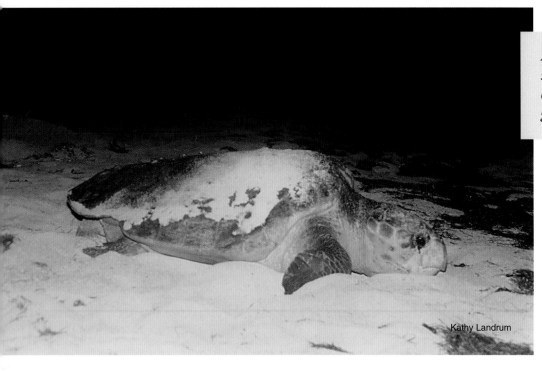

Kathy Landrum

Kathy Landrum

all the eggs hatch, and many hatchlings will not make it past the hungry birds and crabs, on their dash to the sea. Once they finally reach the ocean, fish are also waiting for a meal. In an average year, 15 to 18 thousand baby turtles may make it to the water, but only a small percentage will survive.

Many years will pass before these sea turtles grow to maturity as they cruise the open sea. Once the female turtles mature, they will return to the same nesting area where they hatched to lay their eggs. Juvenile hawksbill turtles are also common in the area, and the giants of the sea turtles, the leatherbacks, which can weigh up to 1,200 pounds, have been seen passing through park waters. All species of sea turtles are protected in the United States. Unfortunately, since they are not protected in many other countries, hundreds of thousands of these ancient animals are taken yearly for food.

REEFS AND FISH

Ancient coral reefs are the foundation of the Dry Tortugas islands, topped by a shallow basin ringed by living coral reefs. Tongue and groove reefs are common on the eastside, and patch reefs and pinnacles are scattered throughout the park. As water levels changed, new reefs developed on top of the old ones. Hard corals, composed of colonies of tiny animals called polyps, cover the outer surface of previous skeletons that formed over the years. They grow in a symbiotic association with algae, which benefits both organisms. Algae grows within the polyps and gives coral its vivid colors; greens, yellows, purples and reds. The algae, called zooxanthellae, provide oxygen, food, and enhance the building of the coral skeleton, which gradually forms reefs. Some of the common hard corals involved in the formation of the coral reefs in the park are star, brain, and staghorn.

Flexible corals are common in the park and include sea fans, sea whips,

National Park Service

and sea plumes. They are often mistaken for plants, as they sway in the currents. These branching corals do not have calcium carbonate to form a hard skeleton, but have polyps that feed on plankton carried by the ocean currents. The beautiful purple sea fan is common along the moat wall at the fort.

More than 450 species of fish have been documented in the park, with 300 closely associated with coral reefs. Many species of beautifully colored tropical reef fish are common, including angelfish, blue tang, sergeant majors, parrotfish, grunts, porgies, and squirrelfish. Larger fish are tarpon, barracuda, grouper, shark, and snapper. The protected spiny lobster and queen conch are also common throughout the park. These reefs, far distant from the mainland, provide some of the most outstanding habitats for fish and other sea creatures in the Florida reef tract.

BIRDS

The Dry Tortugas are a birding paradise, largely because they are located in the flyway between the United States, Cuba, the West Indies, and South and Central America. Hundreds of species of migrating songbirds and warblers arrive in the spring, "dropping in" to rest on their long journey from their southern winter range, to their northern range. Broad-winged hawks, merlins, kestrels, peregrine falcons and other hawks are also seen as they pass through on their migrations. There are also some resident bird populations living and nesting on the islands.

Scientists began to study the area for its unique marine and bird life by the early1800s. The famous naturalist, John James Audubon, arrived at the Dry Tortugas in 1832, and described the bird colony on Bird Key, "On landing I felt for a moment as if the birds would raise me from the ground,

Wes Pratt

A masked booby with a chick on Hospital Key. (left) The sooty terns nest on the ground at Bush Key. When the chicks hatch the parents fly far out to sea bringing back fish and squid for their young. (below)

so thick were they all around, and so quick the motion of their wings. Their cries were indeed deafening, yet not more that half of them took to wing on our arrival.…We ran across the naked beach, and as we entered the thick cover before us, and spread in different directions, we might at every step have caught a sitting bird." The birds he described with their distinctive call were the stark, black and white sooty terns. Sooty terns make their only known nests in the continental United States on the islands of the Dry Tortugas. However, this is not their permanent home. They are "pelagic" and spend their life flying over the ocean returning to the islands only to nest.

Sooty terns can first be heard calling in the night sky sometime during the month of December. Their flock increases along with their continuous day and night chatter until February, when they land on Bush Key to lay their eggs on the sandy bare ground. Most nests consist of a single, cream colored egg with brown speckles, which closely resembles the sand and coral rubble surrounding it. Once the chicks hatch, they are fed by both parents, who may fly out to sea as far as 50 miles in search of small fish and squid for food. This colony of terns number between 80 and 100 thousand during the nesting season, when the islands come alive with the constant, noisy chatter of these remarkable birds.

Once the chicks can fly, usually in late August, the colony completely abandons Bush Key. One day they are suddenly all gone, to return about six months later. Sooties stay in the air over the ocean 24 hours a day for most of the six months when they are gone, covering great distances in their migrations. Some of the birds banded at the Dry Tortugas have been identified as far away as the southern coast of Africa. Upon their return to Bush Key, the adults will nest near the same spot, as in years past. Sooties have been identified to have lived as long as 30 years. Historically, the sooty

Noddy terns, with their distinctive nodding heads also nest on Bush Key. (right)
The magnificent frigate bird, with a wing span of up to seven feet, is a common
sight soaring above the water and nesting on Long Key. (below)

Janet Taylor

terns nested on Bird Key until this island washed away in the 1930s, and they started nesting on Bush Key.

The islands are also the home of nesting colonies of brown noddy terns, masked boobies, brown pelicans, and the magnificent frigate birds. These species of unique sea birds each have their own special place in the park. The brown noddy, with its characteristic nodding head, also nests on Bush Key in the low vegetation. They are much smaller in number than the sooties.

The magnificent frigatebird, with its wingspan reaching seven feet, is commonly seen in the park, soaring above the fort walls to take advantage of the updrafting winds. A colony of frigatebirds nests on Long Key in the mangroves, the only known nesting place left in the continental United States. Another species, the large white and black masked boobies, lay eggs on the sandy ground of Hospital Key. Pelicans are common within the park where they nest on Bush and Long Key and are often spotted at the dock, on pilings, or diving for fish.

SCIENTISTS

Scientists have been attracted to the Dry Tortugas because of the area's wildlife, coral reefs and remote location for many years. James Audubon came on a birding expedition in 1832. Naturalist Louis Agassiz, an expert on ocean fish, followed him in the 1850s. Many other scientists interested in the great natural resources of the Dry Tortugas, including Louis' son, Alexander Agassiz, followed them. In 1881, Alexander Agassiz visited the Dry Tortugas and mapped the islands, seagrass beds, and reefs.

On later trips, Alexander Agassiz was assisted by an outstanding field biologist, Alfred G. Mayor, who suggested a research station be established to study the fauna of the tropics. Mayor also recommended the station be

Janet Taylor

The Tortugas Laboratory established by the Carnegie Institution was constructed on Loggerhead Key in 1904.

marine laboratory in the world.

By 1904, Dr. Mayor had a research vessel built, the *Physalia*. Two prefabricated lab buildings were taken to Loggerhead Key and assembled on the north end of the island. Workers constructed a dock, dock buildings, kitchen and a windmill for pumping seawater to be used in the lab. The laboratory operated during late spring and summer months, when the seas and weather were more calm and cooperative for their research. During peak hurricane season, in late summer and early fall, the buildings were closed and the research vessel either stayed in the sheltered Miami River or was taken on research expeditions to other tropical areas around the world by Dr. Mayor. The only other buildings on the island were the lighthouse and the keepers' kitchen and house.

Long before the use of SCUBA diving equipment, research was conducted at the lab using dive helmets which allowed scientists to stay under shallow water several hours to observe marine life. The scientists also performed the first experimental heart transplants on sharks, and the first underwater black and white photos were taken in 1908, followed by the first underwater color photographs in 1917. By the time the station was abandoned in 1939, over 140 scientists had worked at the Tortugas Laboratory, publishing thirty-five volumes by the Carnegie Institution of Washington, known as the "Papers of the Tortugas Laboratory." Many other papers were also published in other journals. These publications are important today as a scientific record to compare the condition of the reefs and marine life at that time to what is present today.

After returning from a research trip to Somoa in 1919, Mayor was diagnosed with tuberculosis, and spent some time in a sanatorium in Arizona, trying to recover. Three years later, in the spring of 1922, against his

located at the Dry Tortugas, because of "its isolation from the continental land masses, lack of commercial fisheries around the islands, lush reef and clear water." In 1902, the Carnegie Institution of Washington approved the construction of a marine research laboratory to promote scientific research, and chose Mayor as the director of the laboratory. Mayor became a driving force for the scientific study in the Dry Tortugas that began with the support of the research laboratory. Scientists came from around the world to perform research in what was considered at that time to be the best tropical

Alfred G. Mayor, the first director of the laboratory, at the helm of the research vessel Physalia.

doctor's advice, he returned to the marine lab on Loggerhead Key. In June, when wading in shallow water near the marine lab, he fainted and drowned. After his untimely death, the research lab he was so dedicated to continued to operate until just before World War II.

After being abandoned, the buildings and docks began to deteriorate in the hot, humid conditions, and most of the buildings were destroyed by fire in 1964. All that remains today are a few foundations, a cistern, and a monument to Alfred Goldsborough Mayor. The monument designed and created under the direction of his wife, Harriet Mayor, is still there on the north end of Loggerhead Key, and reads:

ALFRED GOLDSBOROUGH MAYOR
WHO STUDIED THE BIOLOGY OF MANY SEAS AND HERE
FOUNDED A LABORATORY FOR THE CARNEGIE INSTITUTION
DIRECTING IT FOR XVIII YEARS WITH CONSPICUOUS SUCCESS
BRILLIANT VERSATILE COURAGEOUS UTTERLY FORGETFUL
OF SELF HE WAS THE BELOVED LEADER OF ALL WHO
WORKED WITH HIM AND WHO ERECT THIS TO HIS MEMORY
BORN MDCCCLXVIII DIED MCMXXII

WILDLIFE PROTECTION

After Fort Jefferson was abandoned by the military, the Dry Tortugas received few visitors. Occasional fishermen and boaters used the safe harbor and came ashore for recreation and to pick through the rubble for souvenirs. The fort sat empty, with the remaining cannons and metal structures rusting away under the harsh sun and salty air. The ghosts of the past were free to roam the deserted passageways and corridors. Attention soon changed from

Janet Taylor

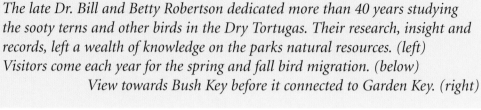

The late Dr. Bill and Betty Robertson dedicated more than 40 years studying the sooty terns and other birds in the Dry Tortugas. Their research, insight and records, left a wealth of knowledge on the parks natural resources. (left)
Visitors come each year for the spring and fall bird migration. (below)
View towards Bush Key before it connected to Garden Key. (right)

a declining human presence, to the unique plant and animal life that lived in this remote island paradise. An Executive Order, signed by president Theodore Roosevelt in April 1908, set the area aside as the, "Tortugas Keys Reservation," a bird sanctuary under the management of the Department of Agriculture, as a breeding ground for native birds.

Later, in 1935, President Franklin D. Roosevelt declared, by presidential proclamation, the area as a part of the National Park Service, to provide for the protection of the historical structures, shipwrecks, artifacts, wildlife and reefs. The park was officially known as Fort Jefferson National Monument.

In 1992, an act of Congress changed Fort Jefferson National Monument to Dry Tortugas National Park. The new legislation was very specific in the protection of the marine animals and natural resources in the 100-square-mile area, in addition to protecting the cultural resources and shipwrecks.

Janet Taylor

Wayne Lan

CHAPTER 8
LIVING IN THE DRY TORTUGAS

People have lived on the islands of the Dry Tortugas since the first lighthouse was built on Garden Key, in 1825. When the area was established as a national monument in 1935, park employees moved on to the islands, and continue to live there today.

Living in this remote, tropical paradise, one's life is certainly ruled by wind, water, and weather. On many windy or stormy days, boats and seaplanes cannot run, so appointments are broken, food and supplies are not delivered, and the mail does not arrive. Boaters sometime get stranded for days in the protected harbor by the rough seas surrounding the Dry Tortugas. Reliable communications to the mainland are never taken for granted.

REPORTS FROM ROBERT R. BUDLONG

Some of the best early descriptions of living in the monument come from a superintendent (custodian), Robert R. Budlong, whose monthly reports to the director of the National Park Service described his two and one-half years at the park during World War II. He transferred from Canyon de Chelly in Arizona to the islands and lived with his wife and young daughter at the fort. His descriptions of life at the fort give insight into the living conditions of the time and his reports were often exceptionally humorous and candid, considering they were part of the official correspondence of the time.

When the boat bringing supplies and food broke down in August 1942, he wrote, "We hear by radio today that the attempt made this morning to run the boat back to the island was not successful, the new engine breaking her tailshaft just one hour's run out of Key West. I believe the boat carried food supplies for us also, and in view of the fact that we have been living on "crawfish" (spiny lobster) for some weeks past, we regret the breakdown of the engine. Anything can become monotonous in time, and did you ever try eating lobster two or three times a day for several weeks? We have lived on it for that time, since we have had little else. But I forget canned milk—we chill it in the icebox and make ice cream of it, so that our diet had consisted of that ominous-sounding combination, lobster and ice cream, for a rather long time. You must come down and have dinner with us sometime. We'll offer you lobster and ice cream…you bring the steak."

Later, he described his attempt to grow fresh vegetables, "Being unable to get fresh vegetables very often, and living mostly on seafood, we hopefully planted a garden. Commander Hoffman, of Key West hopefully donated a hundred pounds of fertilizer.

Those interesting little creatures, the land crabs and soldier crabs, hopefully watched the beans, carrots, tomatoes and lettuce push through the sandy soil, patiently waited until they were several inches high, and then dined sumptuously. We're going to grow petunias in window-boxes."

The hot, humid and salty environment of the Dry Tortugas certainly takes it toll causing damage to equipment and metal structures. Budlong described his views on some maintenance issues, "When we arrived here a year ago we found an automatic chlorinator installed in the water line. It was not in working condition. I think it was called an automatic chlorinator

e fort encompasses almost all of Garden Key.

Wayne Landrum

One of the first buildings during construction of the fort was the engineer's quarters. It was rebuilt in 1939 and today is used for employee housing.

because every time we started pumping water the chlorinator automatically refused to chlorinate. Arrangements were made to exchange it for an electric-motor-driven unit, and this was received during the month. We hope to put this apparatus in use chlorinating the drinking water whenever we get the materials to use for chlorinating the drinking water we hope to collect from the rains, when we get the rains—if we ever get them, you see, our drinking-water problem is not only serious but also somewhat complex."

Humor is always helpful and certainly must have been a necessity for enduring trying times. On engine repair he reported, "Humidity has increased and the rust problem haunts us. Motors quit and demand repairs. One of them lost its muffler during the month. My Man Friday was standing near it while we were pumping water within, and being of a trusting nature he rashly turned his back to the motor and bent down to tie his shoelace. The motor promptly blew its muffler completely off and severely reprimanded

Mr. Russell about a foot south of his waistline."

There were only four people living on the island at the time: Budlong, his wife and young daughter, born after their arrival, and a maintenance worker. Mail service was sporadic, often taking weeks to reach the fort. He wrote, "Reports aren't quite current either. We tear our hair in despair at the receipt of detailed forms that must be filled in, showing the number of cars arriving at the area, when this Monument is located seventy miles at sea, there are no bridges, nobody can get gasoline anyhow and seagoing automobiles are not yet in general use. We receive requests for reports by certain deadlines, and we either receive them after the deadlines are long dead and gone or else we don't have a mail collection until days or weeks later. This report is also going to be delayed—we haven't had a mail collection so far this month and if we have one this week it will be a miracle. We can simplify all this by stating that conditions are normal, everything is going well, and we have everything under control—well, almost. The difficult we do at once: the impossible takes a little longer."

With only two paid employees in the park, each person had to perform many different tasks. Budlong reported, "The island's population was reduced to its usual number, so once again the custodian and his family and My Man Friday constitute the island's only inhabitants, laborers, electricians, ranger, historians, boat captains, marine engineers, lecturers, guides, painters, carpenters, radio operator and technicians, mechanics, landscapers, wildlifers, photographers, plumbers, naturalists, clerks, statisticians, file clerks, stenographers—look, this sort of thing can continue indefinitely, but I think it's tiresome, so let's stop."

Budlong reported monthly on wildlife observations. In June 1944, he wrote the following account on counting the sooty tern population, "I don't

Kathy Landrum

know quite how they do it in the other wildlife regions, where they show their numbers boldly in the usual round figures. Here our methods show precision: we employ the very latest and refined techniques of experts—we don't guess them here, we count them. We row over to the island, and I send forth My Man Friday to ride herd upon the sea-birds, have him round them up together, by their many tens of thousands, all in one big flock he hold them, then past me, one by one he sends them past me. Or he herds them past me flying, and I count them in their passing; one by one I count the sea-birds, for I know our wildlife experts want these figures with exactness. And I almost had them counted, when a ship came in the harbor, passed quite closely by the island, and a blonde stood at the railing in a most breath-taking costume, stood and called and waved and beckoned, and I quite regret to state that I stopped counting for the moment. That was fatal, that was tragic, that completely spoiled my counting, but of course I left there promptly, came back swiftly to the landing, met the ship and did the honors, showed our visitors the island, told them all about the fortress, and I quite forgot my counting, quite forgot to think of sea-birds, though my mind was still on figures yet I did not think of sea-birds. I regret that circumstances interfered with this year's census."

TODAY AT THE PARK

Budlong's humorous reports detailed many problems and situations that are still encountered today. Living in this remote outpost can still be frustrating, aggravating and sometimes tragic, so a sense of humor certainly helps when living in this isolated paradise. Today, there are more employees and families living in the park than when Budlong lived there. Communications have improved and supply deliveries are more consistent.

Kathy Landrum

*Skilled masons repair the weather damaged walls of the 150 year old fort. (left)
A contractor refurbishes and paints the harbor light. (right)*

The biggest change in the last 25 years is the big increase in visitors to the park due to increased interest in the place, better boats, a more mobile population, and better navigation equipment.

National Park employees and their families are the only permanent residents in the Dry Tortugas. Housing consists of apartments inside the fort, in the modified casemates and the engineer's house in the parade ground. The fort population averages about 12 to 15, and increases when additional work crews do special projects, such as fort stabilization. The residence and maintenance areas are closed to the public for privacy and safety issues. The small number of employees have a variety of jobs, including law enforcement, administration, interpretation (giving guided walks and talks and staffing the small visitor center), scientific research, and maintenance of the park equipment and facilities.

Most park employees work in the park for 2 to 5 years, then move on to other assignments in the National Park System. Those working in the park apply to work there, and for those seeking a fairly remote marine paradise, it is a great place to be. Most love it, some quickly grow tired of the isolation and feel imprisoned, but there is always the hope of a pardon.

Just as in the old days, all food and supplies must be brought in from the "mainland" by the park supply boat, which runs the 140-mile round trip each week to and from Key West. Lifestyles can vary, including staying in the park on days off and enjoying fishing, swimming, and diving; or going back to the mainland (Key West) for shopping and entertainment. One must plan out food and supplies for at least a week between deliveries because there are no stores down the street. Fresh water is still supplied by rain (or made from the sea) and stored in cisterns. There is no fresh water, fuel, food, or other supplies available for visitors. Electricity is provided for the fort by diesel

Janet Taylor

Kayaking has become a popular recreational activity for exploring the waters around Garden Key. (left)
White sandy beaches are enjoyed by visitors on Garden Key. (right)
Resident Reef Landrum spends a winter day on the north beach. (below)

generators. Solar power is used to provide electricity at Loggerhead Key, with diesel generators as a backup. There are no dependable telephone links at the park, but satellite television is available, and a satellite pay phone is available for emergencies. It is certainly a more pleasant place to live today when compared to the Civil War when nearly 2,000 people lived at the fort. But it is still a "pack it in, pack it out" kind of place.

VISITING THE PARK

Once frequented by explorers, soldiers, fishermen, mariners and naturalists, it is now the destination for nearly 100,000 annual visitors. Many of these visitors travel to the park to learn about the past and to tour the shadowy ruins of Fort Jefferson. The park is also a wonderful place to dive and snorkel in clear, aquamarine waters that provide a rare glimpse of historic shipwrecks, colorful reefs, and beautiful reef fish. People also go to see the unique bird life that inhabits the islands, or to see the breathtaking spectacle of migrating birds. Other people simply go to relax on the white sandy beaches and enjoy the subtropical paradise.

The only way to get to the Dry Tortugas is by boat or seaplane. After crossing the vast expanse of open water, the first sight of Fort Jefferson gives the impression that it floats on the sea. Coming closer, the low sandy islands come into view, and the clear water exposes the coral reefs beneath the aqua green water. The fort sits atop Garden Key, an island not much larger than the fort itself.

Fort Jefferson is one of the best preserved and one of the largest coastal forts ever built. The brick and stonework is striking, with graceful arches and perfectly cut granite stones. One wonders at the time and detail that went into its construction for a building whose purpose was to defend against

Janet Taylor

National Park Service

pounding cannon balls.

The mission of the National Park Service is to convey the cultural and natural history and the significance of the place, tell its story, and protect its resources. Another purpose is to stabilize the fort and prevent it from being claimed by the sea. Visitors can explore the bastions and casemates, and see the ruins within the fort and the parade ground, and perhaps feel its ghosts along the way as one walks through history. Or one may sit quietly reflecting on the people who have lived there, or those mariners that simply paused briefly on their way through to somewhere else. The place has been one of high drama and emotions, with prisoners, soldiers, and sailors, each with a story to tell, and for many, this was a final resting place.

The moat wall around the fort has a sidewalk that offers an excellent way to see the colorful marine life in the clear, shallow waters, and examine the exterior walls of the fort. There are beautiful white sandy beaches on the island; perfect places for sunning, swimming or snorkeling in the surrounding waters. There is also a small primitive campground for tents, and a small museum with artifacts of military life and a short video on the history of the fort.

Visitation to the park has been increasing for a number of years. The main reasons for the large increase in visitation is daily ferryboat and seaplane service to the park from Key West. These roundtrips make it easy to tour the fort and swim and snorkel from the beaches around the island. The fort, while not crowded like Key West, is a busy place during the late morning to early afternoon. The 100-square-mile park offers plenty of open space for diving, exploring or just relaxing at anchor. At this time, the surrounding islands are open during daylight hours, except Hospital Key and Long Key, which are closed to the public to protect nesting sea birds. Bush Key is closed during the sooty tern nesting season, usually February to early September.

There are many regulations in place to protect the wildlife and cultural resources, so get the latest information upon arrival, or better yet before you go. Information can be obtained from Everglades National Park or Dry Tortugas National Park.

CONCLUSION

The rich 500-year history of the Dry Tortugas has been significant throughout the centuries, mainly for its strategic location in the Gulf of Mexico. The islands provided a safe harbor for passing vessels, and the fort provided protection for the United States as a coastal defense system, protecting its shipping lanes. Serving as a Union outpost during the Civil War, it provided warships a safe anchorage, fresh water and supplies. It was also a miserable prison for soldiers and prisoners alike.

For many centuries, explorers, pirates, and sailors passed through the Dry Tortugas. For some, it was a place to rest or gather provisions of fish, eggs and turtles. For others, it was a mark on the map for their voyage. For many soldiers and prisoners, it was a place they would rather not be. Ships ran aground and sank on the rocky reefs, often taking passengers and crew with them. The place has been like a truck stop along a remote highway, where many people stopped to rest on their journey to somewhere else.

Isolated today, it is a place of beauty, rich in history, a place for birds, pristine ocean wildlife, and solitude. The white sandy islands surrounded by the sparkling, turquoise sea, with its rainbow colored reefs, support a unique collection of marine life. Even though the Dry Tortugas and Fort Jefferson have withstood many natural changes over the centuries, without the care and protection by its human keepers, this masterpiece of masons and Mother Nature could deteriorate to crumbling brick and lifeless seas.

BIBLIOGRAPHY

Bearss, E.C. *Historic Structure Report: Historical Data Section Fort Jefferson 1846-1898.* National Park Service, 1983.

De Wire, Elinor. *Guide To Florida Lighthouses.* Sarasota, Florida. Pineapple Press, 1987.

Hoffmeister, John Edward. *Land from the Sea: Geologic Story of South Florida.* Coral Gables, Florida. University of Miami Press, 1974.

Hurley, Neil E. *Lighthouses of the Dry Tortugas: An Illustrated History.* Alea, Hawaii. Historical Lighthouse Publishers, 1994.

Manucy, Albert E. *Pages from the Past: A Pictorial History of Fort Jefferson.* Homestead, Florida. Florida National Parks and Monuments Assoc., 1999.

Murphy, Larry E., Editor, *Dry Tortugas National Park-Submerged Cultural Resources Assessment.* National Park Service, 1993.

Ripple, Jeff. *The Florida Keys.* Stillwater, Minnesota. Voyageur Press, 1995.

Viele, John. *The Florida Keys Volume 2: True Stories of the Perilous Straits.* Sarasota, Florida. Pineapple Press, 1999.